# Idyll For a Vanishing River

Readers of *Idyll for a Vanishing River* "inhale the starlight" as they're transported along desert trails of seeming-abandon, lead step-by-word into revelations that bound over precipices rippling "like moonlight on a jaguar." No one dies of thirst along this journey of ancient roads mixed with modern enigmas; Alfier carries readers to new understandings of Earth, Life, and Home.

—Karen Bowles, Publisher and Editor of *Luciole Press*

Glass Lyre Press, LLC.
P.O. Box 2693
Glenview, IL 60026

www.GlassLyrePress.com

Idyll for a Vanishing River
Copyright © 2013 Jeffrey C. Alfier
Paperback ISBN: 978-0-9840352-3-6

All rights reserved: except for the purpose of quoting brief passages for review, no part of this book may be reproduced or transmitted in any form or by any means, electronic or mechanical, including photocopying, recording, or by any information storage and retrieval system, without permission in writing from the publisher.

Cover & interior photo: Jeffrey C. Alfier
Cover design: Steven Asmussen
Design & Layout: Steven Asmussen

# Idyll for a Vanishing River

Jeffrey C. Alfier

*...even as in a drought a river will flow, whose source is in the well-springs of far off and undiscernible hills.*

— Moby Dick, LXXXI

# Acknowledgments

Grateful acknowledgment is made to the following journals, in which these poems originally appeared, sometimes in slightly different form:

*Adirondack Review:* "North of the Santa Maria River"

*Border Senses:* "On the Falling Façade of Mission Cocóspera"

*California Quarterly:* "First Frost on Dos Cabezas Peak" and "Aguila, Arizona"

*Concho River Review:* "What We Long for in Desert Towns"

*Crab Orchard Review:* "Travelogue for a Nevada January", "Coda for a Desert Constellation", and "Walking West on East 5th Street"

*Freshwater:* "Our Elevation in the Blue Range Primitive Area"

*The Fourth River:* "Our Sketch of Death Valley"

*Into the Teeth of the Wind:* "Apache Trout"

*The Kerf:* "Desert Farmer at Daybreak" and "On the Progress of Our Wolf Recovery Program"

*Noctua; Windmills (Australia):* "The Beauty of Loss in Eloy, Arizona"

*Northridge Review*: "Nocturne for La Migra"

*Page Seventeen (Australia):* "Ode to Black Horse Feed & Grain"

*Red River Review:* "The Brilliant Blush of Ancient Cottonwoods"

*Reed Magazine*: "Digs in a Prehistoric Seabed" and "An Ending in the Palo Verde Valley"

*Regarding Arts & Literature (RE:AL)*: "Mojave County", "Leaving the Horseshoe Café" and "Cornering the Light Beyond a Braided Stream"

*Southwestern American Literature*: "Abandoned Quicksilver Mine, Not on the Death Valley Map", "Death Valley Interlude: The Panamint Range", "Ranch Hands We Let Go in 1949", and "Sierra del Tigre"

*Tulane Review*: "Beyond Bakersfield"

*War, Literature and the Arts*: "Paleo Warrior at Blackwater Draw"

# Contents

| | |
|---|---|
| Entering the Great Basin | 15 |
| Walking West on East 5th Street | 16 |
| Barn Swallows on the Pecos River | 17 |
| Coda for a Desert Constellation | 18 |
| Our Sketch of Death Valley | 19 |
| How We Spoke Beyond Hanaupah Creek, Death Valley | 20 |
| If You Climb Cutoff Road Alone Beyond Wildrose Peak | 21 |
| Abandoned Quicksilver Mine, Not on the Death Valley Map | 22 |
| Death Valley Interlude: The Panamint Range | 23 |
| Death Valley in Winter | 24 |
| An Ending in the Palo Verde Valley | 25 |
| Leaving the Horseshoe Café | 26 |
| Cornering the Light Beyond a Braided Stream | 27 |
| On the Progress of Our Wolf Recovery Program | 28 |
| Sabino Canyon Arroyo | 29 |
| The Beauty of Loss in Eloy, Arizona | 30 |
| What We Long for in Desert Towns | 31 |
| Our Elevation in the Blue Range Primitive Area | 32 |
| The Brilliant Blush of Ancient Cottonwoods | 33 |
| A Map of San Manuel | 34 |
| San Simon Valley Fossil Hunt | 35 |
| Beyond Molino Canyon | 36 |
| Ode to the Black Horse Feed & Grain Store | 37 |
| Ranch Hands We Let Go in 1949 | 38 |
| Shadow Soldier | 39 |
| Sierra del Tigre | 40 |
| Mojave County | 41 |
| Beyond Bakersfield | 42 |
| Paleo Warrior at Blackwater Draw | 43 |
| Keeping the Faith at *Via Savona Bar* | 44 |
| New Rumors of a Bobcat | 45 |
| First Frost on Dos Cabezas Peak | 46 |
| Nocturne for *La Migra* | 47 |

| | |
|---|---|
| On the Falling Façade of Mission Cocóspera | 48 |
| Aguila, Arizona | 49 |
| North of the Santa Maria River | 50 |
| The Desert Farmer at Daybreak | 51 |
| Apache Trout | 52 |
| Digs in a Prehistoric Seabed | 53 |
| Mammoth Kill Site, San Pedro River Riparian | 54 |
| Bordered Field, Midland, Texas | 55 |
| Centuries on the San Pedro River | 56 |
| Permian Basin Rancher | 57 |
| Downriver, After the Stations of the Cross | 58 |

*for my grandson,*
*Billy Higgins*

## Entering the Great Basin

I'm hiding in this sun like Icarus.
Say it's the beginning of wise madness.
Back in Twin Falls County, all the locals
knew I took a good beating from bad love.

She swore I was wired with half-hearted oaths,
spineless with indecision and cheap beer.
Scowls could arc so finely across her brow –
they rippled like moonlight on a jaguar.

Speeding south until my eyes rhymed with dust,
I left her dark estimates behind me.
Now I wake with desert suns, nothing more
than a derelict in blood and spirit.

Here, I bend freely to boundless contours,
hear the songs of red-tailed hawks purge my angst,
climb limestone peaks that shield me like a child.
I'll read petroglyphs. Or return her call.

## Walking West on East 5th Street
*— Benson, Arizona*

It is spring, and in a town that awaits
the luster of fairgrounds to come alive,

the doors of taverns open early, like strangers
with a promise. Flat-roofed houses yield

to groves of mesquite. Their limbs stretch
streetlight halos into frail shadows veining asphalt

that webs the neighborhood. The trundling
iron of the Union Pacific enters town at a late

hour. Its headlamp startles shacks to burnished
yellow as it floods for mere seconds the frame

of a drunken soldier, home on leave from a long
war. He shuffles through an unpaved alley

like an astronaut scuffing the dust of the moon.
A final blast from the locomotive seems to hew

the world into the past tense. It surmounts cheers
unreeling from a small crowd seated under

the ballfield lighting of a pickup game. A young
hopeful sprints homeward, rounds third, already out.

## Barn Swallows on the Pecos River

I cover the distance between the frantic
asphalt of the highway and the point where,

over gravel, I descend into their uneasy quiet.
They rise from the russet thrall of underbrush,

leap in frazzled birdsong to orbits fluttering
like leaves caught up in dust devils, scripting

themselves against the sun. They fear I've come
to plunder nests – a timeless fowler.

In a slant of flow, the Pecos slips under
the highway bridge, turns bluer than reeling

sky. The swallows and my footsteps catch
a gust off the water, each wing-shadow

and stride slowing, giving way to river, a handful
of russet stones, this brittle chorus.

## Coda for a Desert Constellation

I.

On the scree of Candelerio Peak, he spreads
a sky chart at his late-pitched camp, and merges,
for the sake of stars, into the towering quiet.

Ravens climb through a blade of final light.
As if halted by moonrise, numberless rail cars
stitch a silenced vector through the desertscape.

Twilight brushes far-off cordillera in a fading
caress of incandescence. The Braille of untaken
switchbacks inhale the starlight without him.

II.

Farther north, at a Tonopah hotel window,
a young boy swishes his hand through a galaxy
of dust motes airborne in a beam of truckstop light.

Down the hall, a man touches a woman's shoulder
for the last time. She pours a bourbon, spares the ice.
Her dry rage is a ship with a fire below decks.

Peering out the window, the boy watches the paper
plate held by a homeless woman vibrate in her grip,
as if tonight, wind was only interested in her hands.

## Our Sketch of Death Valley

Throughout the day, we mounted switchbacks
white with salt, thorn-guarded climbs that met
strengthening heat and droughted air, our eyes
squinting past the burnt silence of distance.

We'd camped along the base of a wide net
of gravel that swept downhill from a nameless
canyon, mesquite shading us all night
from nothing but the stars.

This is where the earth widens and tilts
at less than glacial strides, as if being pried
apart by some indolent Poseidon, men
and myth tasting the silence of extinction.

Whatever's beneath us lays embalmed
in strata, burned to the worn trace of a borax
trench astride milling works left
to the weather-beaten typeface of desert,
pulleys and flywheels frozen corsets of rust.

At dusk, we left the falling sun to trawl
a final swath over the salt pan of dead ocean,
dried-up over millennia, its dust leaching
into the afterwarmth of hours as it floated
back to us from the soundless places.

# How We Spoke Beyond Hanaupah Creek, Death Valley

Snowfall lay soft as an opium dream
over the Panamint Range. Untold
elevations below, in the fine-grained
heat of late fall, we mounted boulders
studded with feldspar. What wind carried
and lost melded amid salmon-orange
wings of butterflies edging our silence.

I cut for you a sprig of desert holly, illicit
but vindicated because I said it would grow
back, unlike the bladed crystals you stole
from that small quarry near Warm Springs.

We seized the bright rush of that day, its sky
clear as the eye of God. With a tenuous faith
in our shaky Jeep – parked facing downhill,
we returned west to our seaboard city
lined with lofty sweetgums and maples,
each avenue a slow burial in leaves.

## If You Climb Cutoff Road Alone Beyond Wildrose Peak

> *Keep to trusted paths and tracks.*
> — **Death Valley warning sign**

A sheer of light will thrust an abandoned
rail bed through crumbling shoals
of sun-beleaguered granite, like a lance
through the heart of this late August.

You may witness the jimsonweed slide
its narcotic poison over the remnants
of scattered ballast, leaping a scenic
pullout to drift toward any shadowed

crevice it can find in stone. You could even
follow its torch-white blossoms until
thirst has you wavering like a Dear John
letter, held up to a midday sun, till it burns.

# Abandoned Quicksilver Mine, Not on the Death Valley Map

You approach it thinking something
bright caught your eye. It's just inside

the entrance, framed sunless against
a low hill. Canted like a doorway

in an earthquake, like a mouth caught
in the middle of a last word, the entrance

beckons. All brochures warn against
rotted beams, rabid bats, snakes and drops

worthy of Dante's Circles of Hell.
But you can't help yourself, equal parts

dread, curiosity and excitement fuel
your pace. Until you hesitate, a few

feet off, kick the loose gravel,
lean down for a simple stone.

# Death Valley Interlude: The Panamint Range

Into bonedust air, bright as spun glass,
I began my climb beyond Badwater Spring,
my relief map a broken web of elevations.
Nonhuman tracks over dunes of Mesquite Flat
could warn wanderers even ghosts die of thirst.

The cab of a '61 Dodge is a carapace of rust
shipwrecked in the sun. Desert holly walks
its silver shards of leaves up a dark lava slope.
Wind that slips crossbeams of shuttered gypsum
mines tastes of ancient salt and rainspouts.

Sun drops behind my last switchback
of the day. Constellations transpire one star
at a time, as if surfacing from the sea.
In a cold wind my campfire glows against
foraged carrion in the teeth of a kit fox.

Its eyes follow my hands into the light.

# Death Valley in Winter

Here, Shoshones watched mesquite forests cleared
to build mineshafts that turned refuge for bats.
Starlings came alien, but stayed to scorn
in winter air collapsing all distance.

The white face of ghost flowers – speckled red,
plunge their thirsty roots to another earth.
Where flash floods say never travel alone,
alluvial fans spread slow as mercy.

No back road camping on the valley floor –
not this time of year or any other.
Lightning flashes in a ghost town window.
The nightfall cools a nocturnal hunter.

# An Ending in the Palo Verde Valley

The sun melts early clouds and lights his face.
He's tired as infantry long on the march,
his wisdom a stark road out of Eden
that reared farms on threads of irrigation.
If he lost faith he never let it show
through eighty sweltering years, still humming
some vague old hymn about debt to mercy,
conceding at last those fields he clung to.

Here, his farmstead's chopped into small ranches
before the cycle of subdividing
finally ends in a back-tax auction.
Speculators wait for flood protection
then place calls to anxious developers
whose backhoes heave boulders he never could.
Drill rigs that chew tiers of sand, silt, and clay,
trust the water table's never too far.

# Leaving the Horseshoe Café

I walk the main drag of sundown
Benson. A woman in an evening
dress recedes through a lane
of houses, her figure airbrushed
onto the smoky blue pallet
of evening.

Beyond the last streetlamp,
the desert is hollowed for copper,
named for sun-struck myths
of gold and phantoms in the brute
majesty of distance where a truck stop
thrives.

A Kenworth lumbers past, Ohio
plates, its grill a wind-lash
of extinguished lightning bugs,
the wings of bright butterflies.

## Cornering the Light Beyond a Braided Stream

My mind is lost among monsoon
flowers – blue flax, gold poppies
and lupine that span a cutbank inside
a ghost town rail bed, where wind
sweats chaparral like fear.
A diamondback forsakes its hide
on the splinter of a crosstie,
like sin left behind at an altar call.

An Aztec Thrush sings vagrant
over black humps of Benson
railcars. My eyes trace its flight
till shadows edge away from stone,
robbing silhouettes from lizards,
my vision ending where storms
left deadfall hung in canebrake
along vanished watermarks.

Beyond this thorn-scape my bootsoles
catch, a longing for cottonwood
green might just be hunger to touch
what remains most human here,
where mining towns once rinsed
arsenic in the San Pedro River
while men clocked madness
by the copper in their blood;


or by this hard white sun that swells
till thirst withdraws me through
the rusted sleep of a broken gate,
back to my car baking astride a field
a scarecrow surmounts, a reign over
what grows beneath him in his castoff
shirt and crossbeam arms, hailing
me in a sky of frantic colors.

# On the Progress of Our Wolf Recovery Program

So it begins – the long restoration.
Fifteen per year till they're self-sustaining,

though the captive-born come without that map
guns and footprints burned into their elders.

Regretting bounties our forefathers paid,
we wait for wolves to breed beyond the myth

of infants suckled wild, or Pawnee tales
our Milky Way's just a wolf's last road home.

Scavengers haunt their trails for carrion.
Cherokee true believers won't kill them.

Where campers dream shadows carved in moonlight
kids mimic yelps and draw a like response.

We pound our rude numbers late into night:
how far they spread equals their resilience –

ranging half a county from their birth pack
is just far enough. But if they thin-out,

we'll promptly redraw the prey densities
to the dismay of elk and their kindred

who hope new wolves keep clear of boundaries
where breath gathers on an ancient road home.

## Sabino Canyon Arroyo

Vanished river, I clutch the remnant stones
you stranded in the tread of your leaving.

Now, your dry bed tastes hooves of cloven prey,
creatures that elude a puma tonight.

Such tracks I follow, though my own will fade
like stars in the eyes of a trilobite.

# The Beauty of Loss in Eloy, Arizona
*for Diamond Lil, wherever she's gone*

I've come at last to this limbo between
Phoenix and demented maps of borders…

Late day is gorged with heat as if it leaks
out of the town's cracked doors and busted

windows, even the sky's broken cloud
cover whose storms ordered earth last night.

Wind courses the sere throats of palm fronds.
Hawks ease through torn panels of a cotton gin.

To cool down, I pour absinthe through sugar
onto ice cubes crackling in a glass, dirty

as dust devils that spin their furtive landfall.
Somewhere in the sinking light beyond

the cul-de-sac, an engine fails to turn over.
One more townie's escape sputters out,

as if leaving was a dialect of which this town
alone was native. I look toward the sound,

watch bats lift black against dimming streets,
their silent hunger racing beyond me.

## What We Long for in Desert Towns

From your father you learned a peasant's
faith in work, that merciful decades
with a forgiving wife means time is a plea
bargain between beggars and angels,
that auto shops and stray dogs attend
them all in this town with two truck stops
to blunt what fails on main street, a new
gypsum plant men hope displaces shuttered
cotton gins that laden haulers could reach
from four exits off an interstate that signals
how empty your town really is, how cattle
guards are here for nothing but ghost herds.

Respite from it all comes with county
fairs – corridors of colored lights to dazzle
the dust, amusement rides to spin townies
into gritty air, barkers daring passersby
to pitch balls or rings into thin spaces;
candy apples, funnel cakes, anything
deep-fried and impaled on sticks you're led
to believe can be had nowhere else,
and always the bright signs in gothic letters
for sights 'never seen outside tent flaps'
– 'Bizarre and Exotic Creatures,'
all the caged freaks you could ever imagine.

# Our Elevation in the Blue Range Primitive Area

In wilderness we're like spies for Moses,
scouting out the land's cure in wildflowers
that flood our vision like an anodyne –
vivid refugees from the last ice age
woven from the loom of its memory.

Here, beyond the door of our shipwrecked faith,
Apaches say rain always answers prayer.

Spruce, fir and piñon rise like sentinels
to lift us from the desert's ancient thirst,
fast against the brink of our own eclipse
as if these heights were our only escape,
spring the only season we believed in.

## The Brilliant Blush of Ancient Cottonwoods

With primal intent, a dozen horses
face each point of the compass
like lookouts posted against
the hunger of pumas. Scents
from their bodies rise so tidal
they soak the twilight hours
that catch you unaware.

At night, you listen for serpents
in arid slide through the held-breath
silence of windless underbrush.
A palomino's pale frame dances
under the night-washed
yellow of palo verde blossoms.
She crosses to a cutbank, descends
the soft walls into Pantano Wash.

Building speed into a full run,
distance shades her flight
against the embankment
of the vanished river,
her hooves sparking stone
as if to thrust light into earth.

# A Map of San Manuel

Ore-dumping trains come and go, but you stay
as copper rods seal your fate to smelters,
the sun on your back – hard as acacia.
Tools you wield at the engine house ensure
tracks men lay across this desert diffuse
their paleo-dread of unfilled spaces.

Out here, a lover you claimed in passion
can't replace the wife you really loved once,
but she'll tame your wants long after hers fail.
She's lived here since rail came in 55',
dragged north from Bisbee by her father –
a man deranged from wars and copper mines.

As each day's end retracts light from vision,
the shadows of velvet mesquite distend
and lean over rail yards like bony ghosts.
Soon you'll dream escape down Tiger Mine Road
past beams you laid, beyond trees you planted
that all night long hold their roots to the earth.

## San Simon Valley Fossil Hunt

Like Sisyphus, we'll always endure.
Plodding through sands, we're desert voyeurs
on ground once a forest of hardwoods.
Flowing north into Gila Valley,
extinct fauna runs leagues below us
strewing their disarticulate bones.

Science rebuilds and names the fragments,
artists conceptions becoming flesh
to puzzle children here on field trips:
sabertooths – by punctures found in skulls,
great camels, mastodons. One drawing
looked like an armadillo from hell.

Even though high noon heat scours the day,
kids love it here, away from classrooms.
Shading eyes from mindless depths of sky,
they bug their teachers about lunch hour,
when to queue so they don't miss the bus,
what the names of those bones were again.

## Beyond Molino Canyon

Bound outward on veins of switchbacks
at the foot of summer, my sky is a cobalt sea.
The spindle-thin mesquite in the cloudy
green hunger of drought loiters in silence
as I curve into wilderness, my destination
half-scripted, an aim rustling remote.

Yet to have mounted this far into desert
foothills – the air abrading skin into salt –
I haven't reached whatever was in mind
when I began, at least the cooling shade
of any granite outcrop, a benchmark,
wordless warnings in the petrified stillness…

The path that brought me here is a bleached
silhouette of the one that first summoned me
through this web of ungauged distance
and stone light that floods air I pull deeper
into my lungs. In my halt, sere wind grits and cuts
with a raw sound. I drink from a tepid canteen

at the edge of a thirst that would fade me
like a spent dream, undone in a heat as mortal
and precise as the pleated shadows of hawks
that slope over windfall heaped by a vanished
river. Their orbits are slender dark apertures
penned against a sun more merciful for its falling.

## Ode to the Black Horse Feed & Grain Store

Founded before the last good war,
see how the dark letters fade to dim
on the store's planked siding, how hay

bales on the loading dock await the hunger
of exhausted horses. But most of all, watch
the clerk – the owner's daughter, alert

behind drowsy eyes, steadfast as she slides
the heavy warehouse door open, greets
the thick sweetness of stacked feed

and loads a final pallet for a rancher
going under, his acres near empty,
all mares sold south to a bidder in Oxnard.

Her eyes offer the rancher what they can,
even as a wheat-scented wind gushes to sting
them, lifting hawks into that raw, opening sky.

## Ranch Hands We Let Go in 1949

Our real problem was not wolves but cowboys
laid-off after the year's final round-up
when we released all hired hands in winter.
Out of work, they'd squander wages in bars,

thrive like coyotes and look just as gaunt.
When a heavy blizzard blasted the plains,
they might make a few bucks mending fences
or rescuing some rancher's stranded herd.

One time, we couldn't hire enough of them.
Hollywood thought their lives were all romance.
But screen-made cowboys, pale as mirages,
wouldn't foul their hands with rope burns, or dung.

Hardscrabble, drought, and runaway mesquite
could grind men down like an Exodus plague.
What vaqueros didn't teach them, wind did.
They fret over things that don't bother most:

a hot meal – out of thunderstorms or heat,
blankets to sleep on a picket shack floor,
odd things left behind in the last bunkhouse,
someone that must leave long before sunup.

## Shadow Soldier

At the San Francisco and Blue Rivers
his eyes trace a flight of vesper sparrows
arcing past catacombs of layered rock
above the confluence of river silt.
Some say he drifted over the border
from Buckhorn, leaving rumors in reserve,
with New Mexico police close behind.

When his feet tramped roads where none existed,
Apaches said he was spoiled by a moon
that tracked him once in some nameless jungle,
no more 'faith or fire' to march within him.
But children take him for an old fool now,
his face gnarled as juniper – hard as grief,
and lips stuttering, audible to ghosts.

## Sierra del Tigre

Outside in the arroyo, jaws of pumas gnaw
down to the white gristle of a bull.
Herds of ruminants quit the field.
Light forgets day with the clean break
of a sunken galleon.
Where a field ends, vaqueros crowd
the fresh kill, flashlights and murmurs
sweeping the redness of the open throat,
an eye missing in the ruined puzzle of its face.

All around, grandchildren hear the hum of rumors
pass from lips to ears while in the kitchen
the madrina sits in a breeze from an open doorway,
her widow's dress a starless expanse of space,
her eyes long softened by forgiving too many
sons, too few husbands.

A polished oval rests on the floor
where a table was shifted when a rifle was cleaned.
Horses born last spring begin to grasp
the rare face of sleet
in the shorn mesquite behind the rancho.

Nightfall melds the borders of every shape.
A granddaughter's wildflowers flash between
candlelight and pier glass.
The madrina's fingers reach out
and trace the air to men gathered around her.
These sons, these poor ones, are her life.
She stands to speak, her sable dress
flowing down her body
over and over again, like dark veins.

## Mojave County

Back in Bullhead City, my years faded
to the self-portrait of a stranger.
So I'm playing gone for good this time.
If I make it as far as Flagstaff
I'll call my new luck phenomenal.
Copping a plea with a midnight
interstate, my thumb earns a ride
with a trucker, and we boresight asphalt,
clocking 80 for untold miles till headlights
flash on then off behind us. A formless
gray Mack rockets by. I hear, *gypsy
trucker. Out of hours, over weight limits,
luggin' God knows what in that trailer.
Just giving notice he's overtaking us.*

I know as sure as a roll of snake eyes
not to query what may be in that trailer.
I've long learned to leave wrong enough
alone. But that don't stop me wondering
how many highways the bandit must burn
under the dead-reckon of moonlight,
Dexedrine fueling desire and inertia,
how long he must sweat patrol cars,
if anything will get a chance
to freeze again in his headlights.

## Beyond Bakersfield

He has signed for the keys to a small house
he now owns a block from Armand's
Diesel Road Service, which tows lame
engines and overheated truckers
off interstates that map the valley.

Scanning the beggared Eden of a backyard,
he takes in the itinerant rage of crows
in the sole camphor tree, the quiet
scent of cottonwoods, and the whisper
of windfall apples decaying into the earth.

Inhaling the pungency of wrought iron
and failed gardens, he turns to gaze across
the street; young daughters of a migrant
farmer pull fistfuls of gold poppies, just
to clutch their brilliance, as their mother

sings a ballad that ascends the midday
heat. Her tune will stay with him like the din
from pry bars and wrenches of Armand's
workers; like the silence of all the women
who said they'd never leave without him.

## Paleo Warrior at Blackwater Draw

Near the cold blank stare of an empty cave
he crouches, waits for a seam in the clouds
of a sensuous line of thunderstorms
as lightning fractures the face of ice fields.

Letting the dark labored miles of his mind
unfold before shadows of nine-foot wings,
he summons blooded faith in stone spearheads
– smooth as grinding stones, or a mother's touch.

He thinks the hunt and his tribe unfading,
his fists like condors leaping in the wind.

# Keeping the Faith at *Via Savona Bar*
—Valentine, Texas

I took courage and asked a woman to dance.
Her face had been buried in her hands most
of the night. She was so blue she could've
been stage-lit that way, so I was pleased
she took my offer, and our steps moved
to the Mexican band that plays here every
weekend, vibratos to lure you from solitude
sure as ice cubes exchanged between lips.

A few vaqueros glanced past the door's
rusted swivel, tossed half-spent smokes
and entered, thankful it's a place without
a cover charge. Each one deemed his drink
to be what lets him down easy. My own
choice was a bottle always coated in dust.
It took but a few sips to cause me to amble
outside in the cool late dusk, the chance lost
once more to steal a march on moonlight,
off at last to watch my woman at home
toss in her sleep on my side of the bed.

## New Rumors of a Bobcat

Summer heat floats softly at twilight,
like slumber through an opium den.

She dreams blooded masks of viscera –
an arid reign over cloven prey.

As patient as a votive candle
in plaintive dialects of shadow,

she tracks an unsuspecting heartbeat,
the silent scripture of every breath.

## First Frost on Dos Cabezas Peak

This ground is seasoned by extinct fauna.
The waking moon hunts-down a vanished sea,
dredging arroyos for water traces.
A cougar melds with darkening edges
of nightfall. She takes leave of kestrel wings
climbing winds above San Simon Valley
where moon-lit shadows float across shoulders
of jagged granite and sycamore stands.

In the distance, a collared lizard glides
through labyrinths of a ghost town graveyard.
He waits for dawn to heat his florid skin
as abandoned mineshafts flood with darkness.
I feel the long November night descend.
I pull my blanket as close as a womb
and draw rhythms of air through worn out lungs.
My park brochure begs me to leave no trace.

# Nocturne for *La Migra*

Border towns are places forever shy
of somewhere else.  In La Escondida,
she could touch the future out her window,
this town where myth says a spectral mother
weeps forever, searching for the children
that had drowned in some sleepwalking river.
But local legends can't feed her brothers,
so she gave her body as down payment
to a man with no name, to drive her north
where the truck broke down – her fare depleted.

Crossing the ebb of Rio San Jose,
she pondered life at that meridian,
the wind-seared alluvial plains where Time
leaches isotopes from volcanic doze,
and Navajos heal with songs of water
past the foul afterbirth of mine tailings.
But there were still the migrant camps to find
under the embrace of a foreign sun,
a future hung from a thread of harvests,
the blind horizon daring ghosts to move.

# On the Falling Façade of Mission Cocóspera

Rivers would change their names
for pueblos extinguished
in the smell of ravens,
by roads no more traveled
in the splendor of wind
and ablution of rain.

Transept. Sanctuary.
Walls pitted like smallpox
by dusts of departure,
trace the ghost ship of God.
Time, cup of solitude.
A cup that will not pass.

## Aguila, Arizona

This landscape is littered with spent omens.
The day you were born, passenger trains quit:
towns of four hundred were unworthy stops.
These are things you can't explain to lovers
when back roads are dark islands in sad towns.

You fight the awkward dryness of your lips
as you taste the softness behind her neck,
strong as the soil that welds your sweat to plows
year in and year out, all for bragging rights
for one more round of cantaloupe harvests.

Tears of women you should have never known
will burn like spindrift when you turn away.

As dawn drifts across McMullen Valley,
you wake in a strange house, but lie silent,
hearing footsteps creak against old floorboards,
the way tree limbs in the dark used to say
the time had come to cut the hanged thief down.

# North of the Santa Maria River

To put knives in their thirst, Conquistadors
named rivers for saints, though earlier tribes
once swore this flow was the tear of a god.
This is where the Indian gift shop stands
where you buy your wife turquoise souvenirs
for your twentieth anniversary.

The girl working the counter tells some drunk
another tribe's land-grab makes wind foreign,
while your eyes dream her skin inviolate,
a smoothness tinged like suns ever-setting,
and she haunts your road home to Gila Bend.

What won't hurt your wife is what she can't see:
at night, while she is lying below you,
your mind shape-shifting that Indian clerk
until clenched eyes see another body.

Nonetheless, you finish making love, smile,
say 'I love you', and slide down beside her,
the way it seems it's been done forever,
the mind in traffic of opportune souls
like asps on the breasts of Cleopatra.

## The Desert Farmer at Daybreak

Sleep drags you to the shoreline of your fields.
Your dreams were canarygrass choking wheat.

It's then you stand up slowly on the porch,
face the sun, hardened eyes on the tractor,

your right hand in a far different year
pressing hers softly, staggered at the loss.

This is you, having worked your entire life
never to stagger, overwhelmed by light.

## Apache Trout

Spring means spawning in the tributaries
and legends say willows are a birthright.
Your disguise of ochre and olive skin
melds your compass to the late summer moons
that glint off shades of conifer forests.
Here, your ancestors dreamed six hundred miles
in a profligate span of three rivers
that outsiders stocked with your hostile kin
while men corrupted to indifference
made you a refugee in headwaters.

But you were summoned back by your namesake
long before the grazers and timber men
repented in hatcheries. Natives say
if they build you one more stream, your rebirth
will make history buy back the legends.

## Digs in a Prehistoric Seabed
### —for Walt McDonald

Smokey Hills, Kansas, won't lure romantics,
but we love a frontier of chalky earth
swept for us by ten million years of wind
where hours and seas, retreating forever,
carved pinnacles and spires that shade us well
when we leave the comfort of lecture halls.

No one's lonely for vanished worlds as we,
dragging tools to resurrect extinction:
compressors that feed air scribes and grinders,
old butcher knives swindled for a dollar
from flea markets – used to pry sediment
loose from earth we'll beseech with rock hammers.

Weathered-out from graves of chalky limestone,
we'll hold bones up to sunlight and wonder:
as they swam in a sea owned by dust now,
did their sea-born brains perceive the changes
from tectonic plates shuddering below
as waterways narrowed and mountains rose?

Here, we unearth teeth lodged in spine fragments
from beasts unaware Time would not keep them;
touch each like blind fingers reading a face –
agony's map of vertebrae and jaw,
just gifts you buy at the fossil shop now,
shadows the wind whispered through, and was gone.

## Mammoth Kill Site, San Pedro River Riparian

Ice-age ghosts picket the substrata waking
under the muted radiance of a springtime
desert. Below cottonwoods, graythorn
and mesquite make an ashen reach into wind.
Their spindle-light boughs creak where hikers
built a brush-arbor from the desiccated
timber of a railroad long silenced on its way
to a vanished silver mine. I sit beneath it,
my casual slumber spooked by a wingspan
shadow flashing across my half-open eyes.

Near this place I now raise myself from,
someone unearthed the only bone wrench
ever found on the continent – likely used
to tighten spearheads. It was broken, tossed aside
in a double-extinction, an artifact come across
by accident, illegal to take home if found
today, like anything released from the small
trough I etch in the ground under my heel.

## Bordered Field, Midland, Texas

Fence posts are cobbled from whatever
field hands can gather: gaunt and rotting

branches, signposts fallen on gravel roads
orphaned by the progress of interstates.

Barbed wire suspends them in its tensile
grip. Beneath the lowest strand run

the bright ensigns of lupine, globemallow,
and white butterflies circling empty

liquor bottles that bear the prints
of the fists that threw them.

# Centuries on the San Pedro River

Storm clouds born above the Sea of Cortez
insist rivers gather strength under skies
that old smelters defile. Blurring borders,
birds sing the river past rusted checkpoints.
Soaking the stone-patient roots of mesquite,
it runs north to embrocate the chipped flint
abandoned in fire-hearths of vanished tribes
who cleared earth of mastodon and mammoth,
bequeathing tusks to hunters of relics.

Upstream where you bend west, your name is changed.
Half the continent's bird species stop here
to rest in cottonwoods twisting in wind.
They remind the native thrashers and owls
that borders are illusions, maps a myth.
Humans come just the same. True believers,
we frown over what a river could lose.
Pupfish and pikeminnow vanish from sight.
Our footprints are intent on staying behind.

## Permian Basin Rancher

Wind undercuts all ground and presence.
Anything that breathes is a caravan of heat.
He knows it in the way chronic drought
sears riverbed cutbanks, in the way a young
tanager sings uncovered in the nest, how
Aermotor windmills churn groundwater
into stone tanks. Below the surface,

cylinder pumps become a damp cough,
await the aquifer. The black glisten
of Corriente cattle are ruminants
in the scorch of sun, foraging pump-jack
shadows, the tanager ascendant now
against ever-isolated storms, the hope
that holds him to the earth like undertow.

## Downriver, After the Stations of the Cross

My woman and I have rowed far south
on the Pecos, the day stretched clean
and bright. Sand bars reach up
through a green murk to scrape our canoe.
As I work my oar, she traces the land's rise
up a steep escarpment. Beyond sight,
an animal's dying screech pitches high.
I know the final puma was killed on these banks
early last century, but still I grow alert.
She is alert as well, raises her camera in hope
of sighting red-shouldered hawks soaring
over persimmon, a wild light within her.

Like some disciple scattered in grief
at the crucifixion, I need these fugitive hours.
I'm first among doubters, a Thomas
who'd have filled the spear wound
with my fist, felt its edges, disjunct and raveled
like desert riverbanks. I don't possess
her depth of faith. It is enough for me
that we drift on the current, prove nothing
beyond this water that releases us for a time
from consequence. In this light, we thread
the sere expanse that spreads away
from us, our progress a slow drawl,
our presence nothing more than a drowse
on the world, supplicants of limestone,
gravel and river, all the wearied beauty
we touch together now. This obedience
to stillness. This present mercy.

# Jeffrey Alfier

Jeffrey Alfier is a three-time Pushcart prize nominee, and a nominee for the UK's Forward Prize for Poetry. He holds an MA in Humanities from California State University at Dominguez Hills. Having served 27 years in the Air Force, he is a member of Iraq and Afghanistan Veterans of America. He is author of seven chapbooks, and a full-length book of poems, *The Wolf Yearling* (Silver Birch Press, 2013). He is the founder of *San Pedro River Review*.

www.ingramcontent.com/pod-product-compliance
Lightning Source LLC
Chambersburg PA
CBHW020703300426
44112CB00007B/498